PLANET EARTH

WEATHER AND CLIMATE

By Jim Pipe

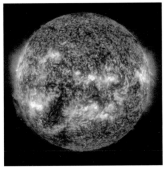

Copyright © ticktock Entertainment Ltd 2008

First published in Great Britain in 2008 by ticktock Media Ltd,
2 Orchard Business Centre, North Farm Road, Tunbridge Wells, Kent, TN2 3XF

ticktock project editor: Rebecca Clunes
ticktock picture researcher: Rebecca Clunes
project designer: Elaine Wilkinson
With thanks to: Suzy Gazlay and Elizabeth Wiggans

ISBN 978 1 84696 516 6 pbk
ISBN 978 1 84696 688 0 hbk
Printed in China

A CIP catalogue record for this book is available from the British Library.

Picture credits (t=top; b=bottom; c=centre; l=left; r=right):
Alamy: 4b, 5b, 19c, 23c, Corbis: 24-25 main, 28 bl. FEMA: OFC l, 5tl. NASA: 1cl, 1r, 4t, 12tl, 26b, 28tl, 29tr, 29cr. NOAA: OFC
c, 22 main. Photodisc: OFC main. Science Photo Library: 20tl, 22bl, 27br. Shutterstock: OFC r, OFC far right, 1t, 1l, 1cr, 3, 4l,
4tc, 5tr, 5cr, 6-7 main, 7t, 7c, 7b, 8tl, 9bl, 10 main, 10b, 11bl, 11br, 12cl, 12bl, 12-13 main, 14tl, 14cl, 14bl, 15tr, 16-17 all, 18tl,
18cl, 18bl, 18c, 20cl, 20bl, 20-21 main, 21tr, 22tl, 24tl, 24bl, 25tr, 25b, 26l, 26clt, 26clc, 26clb, 29br, 30-31 all, OBC all.
Superstock: OFC far left, 4cb, 4-5 main, 9tl, 14c, 18-19 main, 21tl, 22cl. ticktock Media Ltd: map page 7, 8b, 9r, 10tr, 11t, 13r, 15r,
19r, map page 23, 23r, 27t, 27bl, 28-29 main.

Every effort has been made to trace copyright holders, and we apologise in advance for any omissions.
We would be pleased to insert the appropriate acknowledgments in any subsequent edition of this publication.

CONTENTS

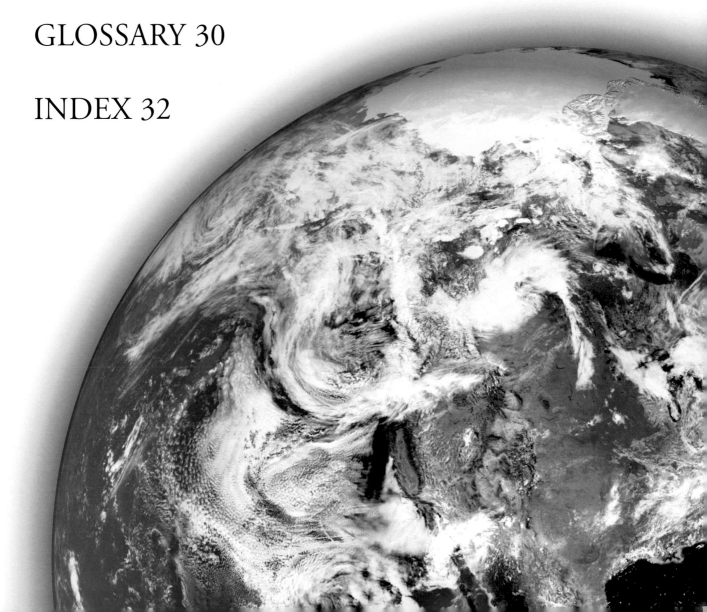

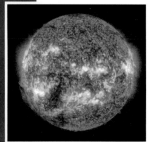

SUN
The Sun's heat is the driving force behind all our weather.

RAIN
Plants rely on rain to bring the water they need for life.

SNOW
Snowflakes form when the temperature drops below freezing.

THUNDERSTORMS
Some dramatic storms produce thunder and lightning.

CHAPTER 1:
The World's Weather

Weather and climate affect how you dress, what you eat and even your holiday plans. The weather can whip up waves at sea and carve the ground and rocks around us. But watch out! Extreme weather can wipe out whole cities, killing hundreds of people and leaving millions without homes.

WHAT IS WEATHER?

Earth is surrounded by a giant blanket of air – the atmosphere. Weather is what's going on in the atmosphere right above your head. It can also be affected by something that happens a thousand kilometres away.

WEATHER SURPRISES

Thanks to modern science and technology, weather forecasts are now fairly accurate, but mistakes still happen. On 16 October, 1987, no storm was forecast in the UK. However, the next day, freak hurricane winds battered southern England – knocking down 15 million trees.

DISASTERS

Weather creates many of the world's worst disasters. Droughts can cause famine when crops and animals starve. Every year flooding causes thousands of deaths. While weather forecasters try to predict when bad weather will strike – when a storm rips through a town, we can only run for cover!

In August 2005, Hurricane Katrina caused widespread flooding in New Orleans, in the United States.

EXTREME HEAT
If your body's temperature rises by 4°C you may be suffering from heat stroke. Without treatment it can lead to brain damage or death. Drink plenty of water in the heat.

LOST IN FOG
Fog is a cloud that touches the ground. It's hard to see very far, and it's easy to lose your way. Fog can be also be dangerous for people travelling by car or boat.

STUCK IN THE SNOW
Snow has changed history on many occasions. When the French emperor Napoleon attacked Russia in 1812, he was defeated by the terrible Russian winter. Only 20,000 out of his 600,000 men survived the journey home.

Plants and animals are adapted to the weather conditions in the area where they live. Buffalo in North America grow a thick coat to protect them from the snow during the winter.

WHAT IS CLIMATE?

When a certain type of weather affects a region of Earth most of the time, it is called climate. The world has many different climates.

Climate affects what plants can grow in an area. The world can be divided into large regions according to what grows there. These regions are called biomes. Soils can also affect what grows in an area. But looking at plants does give you important clues about the climate in your area.

What's it like where you live? Hopefully not too extreme. About 40 percent of us live in temperate climates. These are climates in between the cold polar areas and the hot climates near the Equator. In temperate climates there is rainfall throughout the year and the temperature changes with the seasons.

The saguaro cactus (left) grows in the Sonoran Desert in the USA. During a single rainfall the plant's roots can soak up 750 litres of water – enough to last the plant for a year!

CLIMATES OF THE WORLD

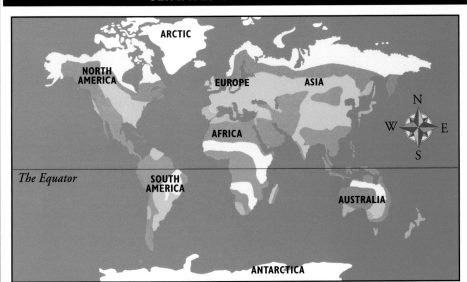

ARCTIC

NORTH AMERICA

EUROPE ASIA

AFRICA

N
W E
S

SOUTH AMERICA

The Equator

AUSTRALIA

ANTARCTICA

MAP KEY

TROPICAL WET
Hot and wet all year round

TEMPERATE
Warm summers, cool winters, average rainfall

DESERT
Dry land with little rain.

TUNDRA
Cold and windy, little rain or snow

TROPICAL MONSOON
Hot all year, with wet and dry seasons

MEDITERRANEAN
Warm, dry summers, mild winters

SUBARCTIC
Cold winters, cool summers, low rainfall.

ICE CAP
Extremely cold and dry all year

WHAT GROWS IN THE WORLD'S CLIMATES?

TROPICAL WET
Plenty of rain and Sun mean rainforests, which support millions of different plants.

TROPICAL MONSOON
Large areas of grassland or savanna. A few trees and bushes grow here.

TEMPERATE
Areas of grassland or forests containing broad-leafed trees, such as oak trees.

MEDITERRANEAN
Tough grass and small shrubs that can cope with the summer heat.

DESERT
Few plants apart from cacti. They survive the dry climate by storing water in their stems.

SUBARCTIC
Large areas of conifer trees. Their dark green leaves absorb the maximum amount of energy from the Sun.

TUNDRA
Plants have shallow roots because below the first few centimetres of ground, the land is frozen.

ICE CAP
Land is frozen all year round so no plants can grow.

HOT IN THE CITY

During the day, buildings are warmed by the air around them. If it is a hot day, they can get quite warm. The materials from which the buildings are made hold onto the heat. After the sun goes down, the air begins to cool off. The buildings slowly cool down giving off, or radiating, the heat they've held. This can make a city up to 5°C warmer at night than the temperature in the surrounding countryside.

SPRING   SUMMER

AUTUMN   WINTER

TEMPERATE SEASONS

In temperate areas there are four seasons: spring, summer, autumn and winter. The different seasons mean changes for many plants. In summer, the leaves of broad-leafed trees, such as oak trees, use sunlight to make food for the tree. In winter, the shorter days mean there is not enough sunlight for them to do this. Losing their leaves saves the tree energy.

THE SUN

It you want to blame the weather on something, blame the Sun. Without it we'd be living (but not for long) on a planet with a temperature close to –273°C. Luckily, the Sun heats our world. It also heats some parts more than others. This makes the air warmer above these areas. Warm air just can't keep still, causing air movements called 'convection currents'. This moving air is what makes the weather change. The uneven heating of the Earth by the Sun also causes water in the air to form clouds, rain and snow.

THE SEASONS

The Sun also gives us the seasons – the changes in the weather that happen each year at around the same time. The Earth takes 365 days, or a year, to orbit the Sun. But it does this tilted at an angle. In summer, the part of the world you are living in tilts towards the Sun, giving you days that are warmer and longer. In winter, it tilts away from the Sun, so the days are colder and shorter.

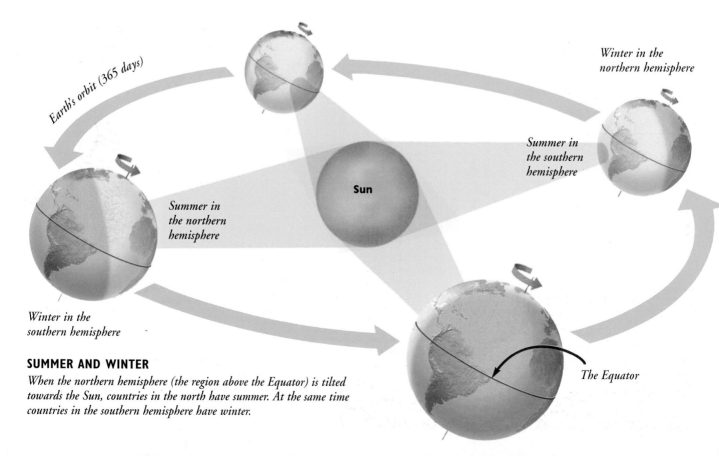

Earth's orbit (365 days)

Winter in the northern hemisphere

Summer in the southern hemisphere

Sun

Summer in the northern hemisphere

Winter in the southern hemisphere

The Equator

SUMMER AND WINTER

When the northern hemisphere (the region above the Equator) is tilted towards the Sun, countries in the north have summer. At the same time countries in the southern hemisphere have winter.

TROPICAL MONSOON SEASONS

Near the Equator, the weather is hot for most of the year. Here there are two seasons – a dry season and a rainy, or monsoon season. These people in Mumbai, India, are trying to save their belongings during flooding caused by heavy, monsoon rains.

DAY AND NIGHT

As the Earth spins around, the Sun seems to move across the sky. This gives us night and day and – you've guessed it – more changes in the weather. In the morning, the Sun rises, warming the ground and the air above the ground. At midday, the Sun is hottest. After the Sun sets, the air cools again.

HOW DOES HEAT FROM THE SUN REACH US THROUGH SPACE?

Materials needed
- Black card
- Scissors
- Pencils
- Modelling clay
- Lamp
- White card

1) Cut two squares of black card.

2) Tape each to the end of a pencil.

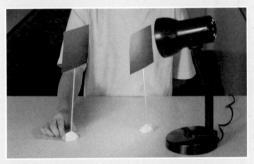

3) Stand the pencils in a lump of modelling clay about 2 centimetres and 10 centimetres from a lamp bulb. Which card is warmer?

Heat from the Sun reaches us by radiation – heat travelling through space in waves of energy. The closer we are to the Sun, the more radiation we get, and the hotter it is.

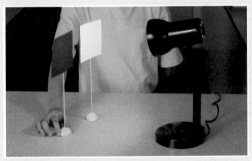

4) Now replace one of the squares with a square of white card. Stand it the same distance away from the bulb as the black square. Which card is warmer?

The white card is acting in the same way as polar ice. White polar ice reflects the Sun's heat away from Earth, helping to cool the Earth.

THE WATER CYCLE

The Sun's heat warms water in lakes and the oceans. This turns water into an invisible gas called water vapour. The rises up into the sky. Here the water vapour cools and turns back into drops of water. The drops fall back to the ground as rain or snow. The rain flows into rivers down into the sea, where the whole process starts again. This is the water cycle. A cycle means something that goes around and around, which is exactly what happens to water on our planet.

Water can create so many types of weather because it can turn easily from a liquid to a gas, or it can evaporate. The amount of water that falls as rain and snow is exactly the same as the amount that evaporates.

The water on our planet gets used over and over again. The raindrops falling on your head contain the same water that fell on the dinosaurs over 65 million years ago.

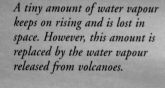

A tiny amount of water vapour keeps on rising and is lost in space. However, this amount is replaced by the water vapour released from volcanoes.

POLAR ICE

When it gets very cold, water turns into solid ice. Most of the world's ice is found at the poles, and there's a lot of it! Antarctica is bigger than Europe, and covered in ice over one and a half kilometres thick. Water held in the form of ice can't go through the rest of the water cycle unless the ice melts.

If global warming causes the ice at the poles to melt, that water will be added to what is already in the oceans. Areas near the sea will be flooded.

HOW THE WATER CYCLE WORKS

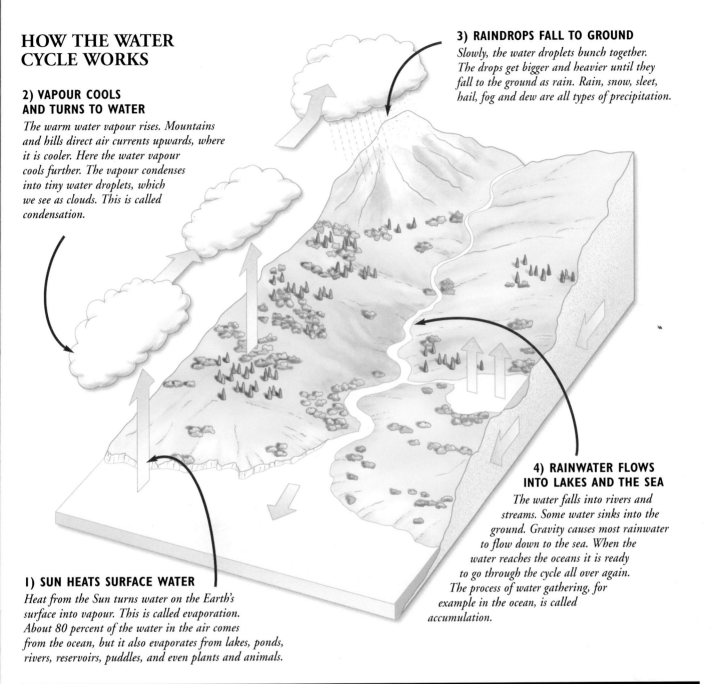

2) VAPOUR COOLS AND TURNS TO WATER

The warm water vapour rises. Mountains and hills direct air currents upwards, where it is cooler. Here the water vapour cools further. The vapour condenses into tiny water droplets, which we see as clouds. This is called condensation.

3) RAINDROPS FALL TO GROUND

Slowly, the water droplets bunch together. The drops get bigger and heavier until they fall to the ground as rain. Rain, snow, sleet, hail, fog and dew are all types of precipitation.

4) RAINWATER FLOWS INTO LAKES AND THE SEA

The water falls into rivers and streams. Some water sinks into the ground. Gravity causes most rainwater to flow down to the sea. When the water reaches the oceans it is ready to go through the cycle all over again. The process of water gathering, for example in the ocean, is called accumulation.

1) SUN HEATS SURFACE WATER

Heat from the Sun turns water on the Earth's surface into vapour. This is called evaporation. About 80 percent of the water in the air comes from the ocean, but it also evaporates from lakes, ponds, rivers, reservoirs, puddles, and even plants and animals.

WATER FACTS

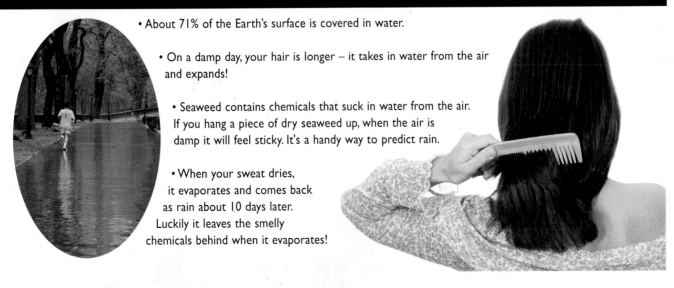

• About 71% of the Earth's surface is covered in water.

• On a damp day, your hair is longer – it takes in water from the air and expands!

• Seaweed contains chemicals that suck in water from the air. If you hang a piece of dry seaweed up, when the air is damp it will feel sticky. It's a handy way to predict rain.

• When your sweat dries, it evaporates and comes back as rain about 10 days later. Luckily it leaves the smelly chemicals behind when it evaporates!

THE PARTS OF THE ATMOSPHERE

THE EXOSPHERE

This layer begins 500 kilometres above Earth's surface. The exosphere is the thin uppermost layer where our atmosphere merges into space.

THE THERMOSPHERE

80–500 kilometres above Earth's surface. The International Space Station orbits Earth in the thermosphere.

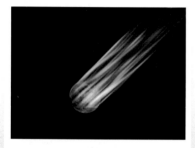

THE MESOSPHERE

50–80 kilometres above Earth's surface. Millions of meteors bump into the Earth's atmosphere every day and burn up in the mesosphere. You see them as shooting stars!

THE STRATOSPHERE

10–50 kilometres above Earth's surface. The stratosphere contains the ozone layer which cuts out most of the Sun's dangerous rays.

THE TROPOSPHERE

Up to 10 kilometres above Earth's surface. This is the place where almost all weather happens.

CHAPTER 2:
Everyday Weather

Have you ever had to fasten your seatbelt on a plane? The bumps you can feel are turbulence – pockets of air moving about. They're part of a giant weather machine that stretches around the whole planet. This machine is driven by the Sun's energy and the oceans, which store lots of heat (like a giant hot water bottle).

AIR MASSES

The Sun and oceans heat up some places more than others, so the air in these places is wetter or warmer than air elsewhere. Giant clumps of this warm wet air, called air masses, are always on the move – changing the weather where you live.

The proportion of gases in the atmosphere changes as you go higher. Mountain climbers have to cope with altitude sickness caused by less oxygen on mountains over 3,000 metres high.

COLD AIR FALLS

WARM AIR RISES

BLOWING HOT AND COLD

When the Sun heats up the ground, this in turn heats up the air above it. This warm air expands and becomes less dense, allowing it to rise upwards. Up in the atmosphere, the warm air cools. It becomes more dense and gravity causes it to move back down to the ground again. This non-stop movement of warm and cold air sets up a cycle known as convection.

If they didn't spread the Sun's heat around, the hot places would get hotter, and the cold places would freeze. In fact, nothing could live on Earth – including you!

FLYING HIGH

The atmosphere is a mixture of gases made up of five layers. Together, the layers stretch 900 kilometres into space. Weather only happens in the layer nearest Earth. This is called the troposphere. Planes going on long trips fly right at the top of the troposphere, above the clouds. This helps them to avoid turbulence.

GASES IN THE ATMOSPHERE

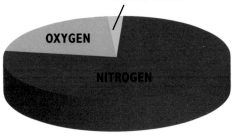

OTHER GASES

OXYGEN

NITROGEN

■ 78% of the atmosphere is nitrogen

■ 21% of the atmosphere is oxygen

1% is made up of other gases, including water vapour

HOW DOES HOT AIR RISE UP THROUGH COLD AIR?

Materials needed
- Glass
- Hot and cold water
- Food colouring
- Clingfilm
- Rubber band
- Large glass container
- Skewer

1) Fill a glass with hot water. Then add some food colouring to help you see the water moving more easily.

2) Cover the glass with clingfilm and secure it with a rubber band. Put the glass inside the large container.

3) Fill the container with cold water until the water level is well above the glass.

4) Poke a hole in the clingfilm with the skewer and watch what happens to the coloured water.

Warm water rises through cold water, just as hot air rises through cold air. This experiment shows how convection currents work.

A WORLD OF WIND

JET STREAMS

World War II pilots flying high sometimes found themselves going nowhere thanks to high-speed winds (up to 400 kilometres per hour) blowing in the opposite direction. Today pilots try to fly in the direction of jet streams. This gives the plane extra speed and saves fuel!

SEA BREEZES

In summer, cool breezes blow inland from the sea. The land is warmer than the sea, and as warm air rises above the land, cool air rushes in from the sea to take its place.

WINDS THAT FREEZE

The stronger the wind, the more quickly your body loses heat. This is known as the windchill factor. Every extra 2 kilometres per hour in wind speed means your body drops 1°C in temperature.

PREVAILING WINDS

Winds that tend to blow in the same direction are called prevailing winds. Trade winds blow east to west across the Atlantic Ocean. These reliable winds helped early European traders sail to America.

WIND

There's over five million billion tonnes of air in the atmosphere. In fact, all that air pressing down on your head and shoulders is about one tonne – the same weight as a car! When the Sun or oceans heat the air, they cause differences in air pressure. This makes air masses move around which is what you feel on the ground as wind.

Air pressure squeezes you all over, but you don't get crushed thanks to the air pressure inside your body. When your ears pop, it's because the pressure outside has changed too fast for your ears to adjust quickly enough. Don't worry – just hold your nose and snort.

A strong wind can make it hard to stand up – it can also give you a very bad hair day!

Tiny grains of sand carried by the wind can wear away rocks. This erosion can cause strange shapes.

MOVING AIR PRESSURE

Think of how a balloon whizzes around when you let the air out. The air inside is moving from an area of high pressure (inside the balloon) to an area of low pressure (outside the balloon). In the atmosphere, when warm air rises, it creates an area of low pressure. Cold air, which is denser, sinks down, creating high pressure. When the pressure is high, the weather is usually sunny. Low pressure often brings rainy or snowy days.

IN A SPIN

The world's winds move in a set way around the globe. Hot air near the Equator heats up, rises and moves towards the cold poles. Cold air at the poles moves toward the Equator. This is an example of convection at work.

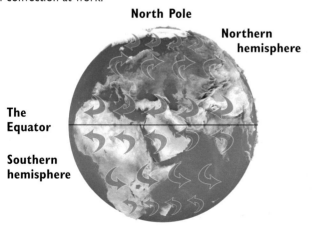

North Pole

Northern hemisphere

The Equator

Southern hemisphere

South Pole

However, the spin of the Earth makes these air masses curve and spin too. Winds rotate counterclockwise in the northern hemisphere and clockwise in the southern hemisphere. This is known as the Coriolis Effect.

HOW DOES AIR CHANGE IN DIFFERENT TEMPERATURES?

Materials needed
- 2 Balloons
- 2 Containers wider than the bottles
- 2 Plastic bottles
- 2 Rubber bands

1) Place two deflated balloons over the tops of two plastic bottles. Use a rubber band to secure them tightly.

2) Place the bottles in the containers. Fill one container with ice cubes and the other with hot water (be careful). What do you observe happening?

> ⓘ **When air gets warm, it expands which inflates the balloon. Cool air contracts, causing the other balloon to shrink.**

CLOUD GALLERY

NIMBOSTRATUS
A familiar blanket of low, dark rain clouds – expect a steady downpour!

STRATOCUMULUS
A big sheet of low-lying cloud with a more lumpy shape than nimbostratus.

CUMULONIMBUS
Brace yourself – these storm clouds stretching high into the atmosphere often bring heavy rain and lightning.

BAD AIR DAY

City smog is a manmade weather condition. The term smog was first used in London in the early 1900s to describe a mixture of smoke and fog. Smog is caused by pollution from vehicle exhausts, power plants and factories reacting with sun and heat. This produces the thick haze we sometimes see hanging over our cities. Smog can make it hard to see, but it also causes health problems, from stinging eyes to severe breathing difficulties.

CLOUDS

As they float across the sky, clouds look as light as a feather. Don't be fooled though – an average cloud weighs as much as a jumbo jet! Luckily for us, this weight is spread out so rising warm air keeps a cloud up in the sky. Clouds are made up of millions of tiny droplets of water or ice, which are so small they can float in the air.

Clouds form when warm air rises. High in the sky, the invisible water vapour cools and turns into water droplets. A cloud's shape and height can help you predict the weather.

Clouds form at many different levels. We call clouds that hang close to the ground mist or fog. Some clouds are as high as 12,000 metres up – higher than Mount Everest.

CUMULUS
Fluffy white clouds often seen floating across the sky. Enjoy the good weather!

ALTOCUMULUS
Round clouds in patches – a sign of unsettled weather to come.

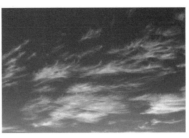

CIRRUS
High white wispy clouds that look like candy floss. Often the first clouds to form along a weather front.

FRONTS

When two giant air masses bump into each other, they take a while to mix. A boundary forms between them, known as a front. Clouds often form where a warm air mass meets a cold air mass.

THUNDERSTORMS

The air whizzing around inside a storm cloud can create lightning. This is a huge surge of static electricity that leaps from the bottom of the cloud to the ground. As the lightning rushes through the air, it produces a shock wave that you hear as thunder. Thunderstorms are most common in tropical rainforest areas. In temperate regions they are most frequent in the summer.

Lightning is hot stuff. The air around a lightning bolt reaches an incredible 33,000ºC when it strikes!

Lightning causes many forest fires each year. This is one of nature's ways of clearing dead leaves and overgrown areas. Some plants, such as the bishop pine, actually need intense heat for their seeds to sprout.

RAIN CHECK

DOWNPOUR

During a storm, over 3 centimetres of rain can fall in 15 minutes. At any moment, there are around 2,000 thunderstorms going on somewhere in the world.

MONSOON

In tropical regions, such as India and South East Asia, there is a rainy season and a dry season. These can cause floods and then drought. In 2005, monsoon rains killed 1,000 people in Mumbai, India, when 94 centimetres of rain fell in just 24 hours.

ACID RAIN

Acid rain occurs when poisonous gases, such as sulphur dioxide from power plants and cars, combine with water in the air. Acid rain eats away at stone buildings and poisons trees, rivers and lakes.

RAIN

By the time clouds form, water is well on its way to becoming rain. The tiny water droplets in a cloud cluster together to form bigger drops. When the drops get too heavy, they fall to the ground. It takes about a million cloud droplets to make one raindrop. But all those raindrops add up. Enough rain falls on Earth every day to fill several hundred bathtubs of water for every person on the planet!

When you face a rainbow, the Sun will be behind you, directly opposite the rainbow. If you try to chase the rainbow, it will seem to be moving with you. You will always be between the Sun and the rainbow!

FREAKY RAIN

Strong air currents have been known to sweep frogs, spiders, fish and even turtles and snakes up into the air. In August 1918, hundreds of tiny fish fell in Sunderland, UK, during a thunderstorm.

WHAT SORT OF RAIN?

Raindrops come in different shapes and sizes. Drizzle is a fairly steady, light rain with raindrops that are about 0.5 millimetres across. The raindrops that fall in a heavy downpour can be up to 8 millimetres across.

CHASING RAINBOWS

Rain and sunshine can combine in the most beautiful way. The Sun's white light is actually made up of different colours: red, orange, yellow, green, blue, indigo and violet. A rainbow is caused by light rays from the Sun being separated into these colours when they pass through raindrops or spray.

Ice crystals in very thin cirrus clouds can cause coronas (bright rings) around the Sun or Moon.

CREATE YOUR OWN RAIN

Materials needed
- Clear plastic bottle
- Ice cubes
- Hot (but not boiling) water

1) Fill a clear plastic bottle with hot water.

2) Leave the hot water in the bottle for a few seconds, then pour half of the water out.

3) Next place an ice cube over the bottle's opening. Watch what happens.

The ice cube cools the water vapour in the bottle. It condenses on the side of the bottle. Water droplets form in the same way.

ICY DANGERS

GIANT HAILSTONE

During a violent hailstorm in June, 2003, the largest hailstone in American history fell on Aurora, Nebraska. The hailstone had a circumference of 47.5 centimetres. The hailstone is being preserved in the National Center for Atmospheric Research in Boulder, Colorado, USA.

FREEZING RAIN

When the Great Ice Storm struck Canada in January 1998, heavy rain followed by frost made electric cables snap under the weight of the ice. Four million people were left without electricity in the middle of winter.

WHITEOUT

During whiteouts the air is so thick with snow you can't tell the ground from the sky. People lose their sense of up, down, far and near. Planes crash and even birds fly into the ground. Sudden blizzards have even buried trains under heavy snow.

SNOW

When you complain about the cold, remember that 20,000 years ago, much of North America and Europe were covered in a layer of ice three kilometres thick. The world has warmed up since then but very cold weather still brings all sorts of hazards.

When the air temperature drops below freezing, water droplets turn into ice crystals. As more water then freezes on the ice crystals, they grow bigger. As these crystals tumble down through the clouds, they knock into other crystals and form snowflakes.

If the ground temperature is above freezing, snowflakes partly melt as they fall, turning to sleet.

Frost is water vapour in the air that turns into ice crystals when the temperature drops below 0°C. It forms an icy layer on the ground that can kill plants.

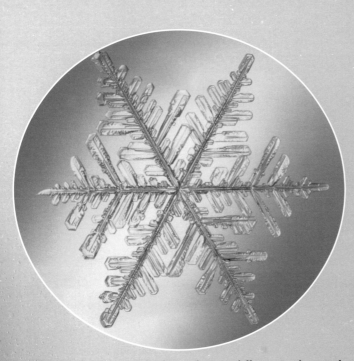

All snowflakes have six sides, but each one is different. Its shape and size depends on the temperature and the amount of moisture in the cloud. The largest snowflakes are around five centimetres across.

HAILSTONES

Most hailstones are the size of a pea, but they can be the size of a golf ball – or bigger! A hailstone forms when an updraft carries a water droplet above the freezing level in a storm. The droplet freezes into ice. The tiny hailstone starts to drop down, but then an updraft takes it back up again and it gets coated with another layer of ice. This keeps happening until the hailstone gets too heavy to rise up and it falls from the sky. If you chop a hailstone in two you can count the layers of ice.

DESERT WHIRLWINDS
Dust devils are small whirlwinds that often occur in deserts.
They are mostly harmless and many are only a few metres high.

WATER TORNADOES
Water spouts are tornadoes that occur over water. Some are over 100 metres wide. Like all tornadoes, water spouts only last a few minutes.

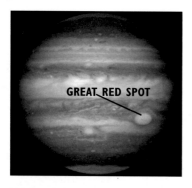

GREAT RED SPOT

STORMS IN SPACE
Earth is not the only planet in the solar system that has storms. The Great Red Spot on Jupiter is a massive storm up to 25,000 kilometres across. It has been raging for at least 300 years.

CHAPTER 3:
Extreme Weather

Most of the weather we experience is fairly ordinary: it's sunny, cloudy, rainy or snowy. But once in a while, parts of the world experience severe weather. Hurricanes, tornadoes and floods cause massive destruction and lead to many deaths each year.

HURRICANES

A hurricane starts life as an ordinary tropical storm. Then heat from the sea warms the air further. Warm, wet air rises rapidly, sucking in more air. The spin of the Earth causes the storm to spin upwards around a centre, called the eye. When the rising air cools, it creates huge rain clouds. Hurricane winds, of up to 250 kilometres per hour, can flatten houses and the heavy rains lead to flooding.

TORNADOES

Smaller, but equally scary, are tornadoes – vicious funnel-shaped storms which spin down from thunderclouds. The largest tornadoes are about one kilometre wide, and their winds can reach speeds of 480 kilometres per hour. Thankfully, they only last a few minutes.

NAME THAT STORM

Giant tropical storms have different names depending on where in the world they form.

Giant storms in the Pacific Ocean are called typhoons.

Giant storms are known as hurricanes in the Atlantic Ocean.

In the Indian Ocean, giant storms are known as cyclones.

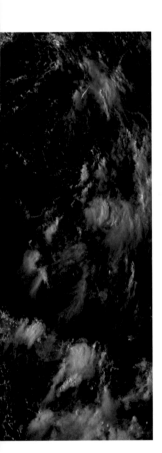

A big hurricane can be as large as Australia, and up to 10 kilometres high. This satellite image shows Hurricane Katrina, approaching Louisiana in the USA, in 2005.

TORNADOES

Tornadoes begin when air inside a thundercloud starts to spin. The whirling air spins faster and faster and sucks warm air up from the ground. The warm air cools and forms a spinning funnel-shaped cloud. When the cloud touches the ground, the tornado sets off at speeds of up to 100 km/h. It smashes everything in its path. It can even lift trees metres into the air.

WHY ARE TORNADOES SHAPED LIKE A FUNNEL?

Materials needed
- 2 Large plastic bottles
- Cold water
- Food colouring
- Waterproof tape

1) Half fill a large plastic drinks bottle with water. Add food colouring to help see what is happening more clearly.

2) Put some tape over the bottle opening and poke a small hole in it. Now firmly tape the empty bottle to the bottle containing the water as as shown.

3) Turn the full bottle upside down. Then begin turning it around in your hand to set the water spinning. Hold the bottom bottle tight.

4) Stop turning the bottle. What happens?

The water in the bottle acts like the air in a tornado. Once it starts, the water keeps on spinning for some time. This is why tornadoes are always shaped like a funnel.

EXTREME WEATHER RECORD BREAKERS

HOTTEST TEMPERATURE
In 1922, the temperature in Al'Aziziyah in Libya reached 58°C.

COLDEST TEMPERATURE
The coldest temperature ever recorded was −89.2°C. This was recorded at the Vostok Research Station, Antarctica, in 1983.

WETTEST PLACES
Cherrapunji in India is one of the wettest places on Earth. It receives an annual rainfall of around 11.5 metres thanks to the monsoon rains. Once it rained over nine metres in one month!

DRIEST PLACE
The Atacama Desert in Chile spreads for 80,000 square kilometres. There has never been any rainfall recorded in parts of this desert.

STRONGEST WIND
The highest non-tornado wind gust ever was recorded on Mount Washington in the USA on 12 April 1934. It blew at 372 kilometres per hour.

FLOODS

The heavy rain that falls during a storm often causes more damage than the wind. Floods sweep across the ground, washing away crops, vehicles and even houses. In 1887, the Huang Ho river in China burst its banks. Around two million people died. Many were drowned, while others died from starvation and disease after the disaster. Heavy floods also result from ocean waves, called storm surges, pushed onshore by an advancing hurricane.

Sometimes when rain falls hard and fast, the ground cannot soak up the water fast enough. This is called a flash flood.

In 2005, hundreds of people were killed by a mudslide in the village of Panabaj, Guatemala. Days of torrential rain, following a hurricane, caused tonnes of mud to crash down the slopes of a volcano burying the village.

MUDSLIDES

Torrential rains can also cause a massive flow of mud –
a mudslide. Sometimes the ground becomes so
saturated it cannot hold any more water. If the
saturated ground is on a slope, the overflow rushes
downhill, sweeping away anything in its path.

DROUGHTS

Across the world different areas get different amounts
of rain. But sometimes an area will receive less rain
than usual, or no rain at all. This is called a drought.
Without enough rain, people and their animals have
no drinking water and crops cannot grow. This can
lead to famine.

*During a drought, wild animals may die from a lack
of food and water. Dry, cracked soil can be whipped
up into dust storms, and dry plants and trees are in
danger of catching fire.*

DUST STORMS

During a large storm, clouds of fine
dust may be lifted to heights of over
three kilometres, then carried for
thousands of kilometres. Sand storms
such as the Haboob in Arabia and
Africa can move entire sand dunes.
These vast walls of dust can strip the
paint off a car!

THERMOMETER
A thermometer is used to measure temperature.

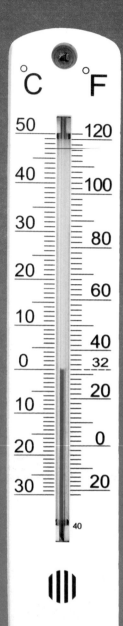

WIND GAUGE
A wind gauge measures the strength and direction of the wind.

RAIN GAUGE
Scientists use a rain gauge to measure the amount of rainfall.

BAROMETER
A barometer shows air pressure.

CHAPTER 4:
Weather Watchers

Today's weather forecasts are more accurate than ever before. Millions of measurements are taken every day to record temperature, wind speed, air pressure and rainfall. In some places, measurements like these have been taken for hundreds of years, which helps scientists to discover if our climate is changing.

THE SCIENCE OF WEATHER

Information to predict the weather comes from weather stations on land, weather buoys at sea and weather balloons high in the sky.

Weather scientists, called meteorologists, use supercomputers, such as 'Earth Simulator' to predict changes in global weather patterns due to climate change. The building that houses 'Earth Simulator' is built on rubber supports to protect it during earthquakes.

RADAR

Meteorologists use radar to track the speed and direction of rain clouds and wind, to find out how heavily rain is falling. They even use radar to track hurricanes. Radars send out radio waves which are reflected back by objects, including storms.

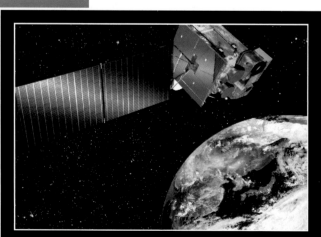

SATELLITE IMAGES

Meteorologists gather lots of data from weather satellites orbiting the Earth. The satellites photograph clouds, snow cover and dust storms. They also take infrared photos which show the temperature of the oceans and the land. Studying the photos over time gives scientists lots of information about weather patterns.

Some computers use data to predict the weather for the week over a wide area. Others, such as IBM's 'Deep Thunder' can create forecasts that pinpoint dangerous flash floods and freezes.

A weather balloon is an inexpensive way to carry instruments up into the atmosphere to measure air pressure and temperature. Computers on the ground track the balloon to measure wind speed.

WEATHER MAPS

- Weather maps can show high and low pressure systems, temperatures and wind direction.
- Computers can create weather maps that forecast periods of 10–14 days in advance to guide human weather forecasters.

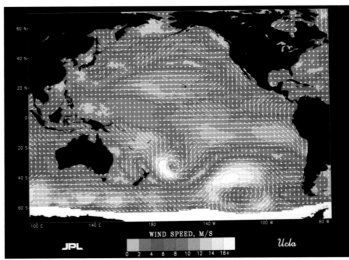

WIND SPEED AND DIRECTION MAP
- This map shows wind speed and direction over the Pacific Ocean.
- The arrows show wind direction.
- The colours show wind speed from blue to yellow. Blue areas are winds with speeds of 3–14 km/h. Yellow areas are winds up to 70 km/h.

GOOD GASES

Temperatures on Mars average around −60°C. Without our greenhouse gases, Earth's climate would be similar. We need some greenhouse gases − it is the increase that is worrying scientists.

GLOBAL WARMING

Hold onto your seat − it's going to be a bumpy ride! The future looks set to get stormier as the world's climate warms up. The Earth's climate has got hotter and colder throughout history, but most scientists now believe it is heating up faster than ever before.

Scientists can't agree how much warmer the Earth will get − perhaps 2°C by 2050. This doesn't sound like much, but if the polar ice caps start melting on a large scale, sea levels will rise. This will create a big risk of flooding to many coastal towns and cities.

HOW DO WE KNOW?

Layers of ice dating back hundreds of thousands of years are frozen on Antarctica. Gases and chemicals trapped in the ice can give scientists important information about how greenhouse gases have affected the Earth in the past. Scientists collect 'cores' of ice that can be studied like icy timelines of Earth's climate.

GREENHOUSE GASES

Gases such as carbon dioxide, methane and water vapour do an important job. They trap heat from the Sun and keep our planet at the correct temperature for life. However, for the past 200 years, people have been using more and more energy. Gas-guzzling cars and power stations create huge amounts of carbon dioxide. This traps more and more heat from the Sun. This gives weather systems more energy, creating more heavy rain and stronger winds.

WE CAN MAKE A DIFFERENCE

One way we can all help to change this situation is to use less energy. Then power stations will burn less fuel, such as coal and oil, which give off greenhouse gases. We can also make simple changes in our everyday lives, such as walking or cycling instead of using the car.

By planting trees we can help nature soak up the extra carbon dioxide in the atmosphere.

EFFECTS OF GLOBAL WARMING

RISING SEA LEVELS
Melting glaciers at the poles will lead to rising sea levels, perhaps as much as a one metre sea level rise by 2100. That's a serious problem for low-lying places such as the Maldives. This group of islands are just 1.6 metres above sea level.

LOSS OF PROTECTIVE ICE
Melting ice caps will also increase global warming. Snow and ice usually form a protective, cooling layer over the polar regions. When that covering melts, the Earth absorbs more sunlight and gets hotter.

The images below show how the amount of sea ice at the Arctic during the summer is decreasing.

SUMMER 1979–1981

SUMMER 2003–2005

EXTINCTION
Polar bears hunt seals on the Arctic sea ice. If the ice cap disappears, polar bears will lose their hunting ground and become extinct.

GLOSSARY

accumulation This is the process of something building up slowly. For example, snow piling up on top of a glacier, water collecting in the oceans, or water freezing into thicker and thicker layers of ice.

air pressure A force created by the weight of air pressing down on the Earth's surface.

atmosphere The thick layer of air that surrounds the Earth. The gases that make up Earth's atmosphere include nitrogen (78%) and oxygen (21%). There is also water, and small quantities of other gases such as argon, greenhouse gases and carbon dioxide.

biomes Large regions that share the same distinctive groups of plants and animals that are adapted to that region's climate.

carbon dioxide (C0²) A colourless, odourless gas present in Earth's atmosphere. It is produced naturally when humans and animals breathe out. It is also produced by burning fossil fuels, such as coal and oil.

climate The average weather in an area over a long period of time.

condensation The process by which a gas changes to a liquid. For example, when water vapour turns into droplets of water.

convection A way that heat moves from one area to another. During convection cool air sinks down and warm air rises. This creates currents in the air that we feel as wind. Convection causes clouds, rains and thunderstorms.

cyclone The name for a giant tropical storm (hurricane) when it occurs in the Indian Ocean.

drought An unusually long period without rainfall. Droughts often cause severe water shortages and famine.

evaporation The process by which a liquid changes to a gas. For example, when liquid water turns to water vapour.

famine A severe shortage of food that can lead to starvation and disease.

glacier A huge, slow-moving river of ice (usually around 30 metres thick). The glacier moves slowly down a slope or valley. Some glaciers move only a few centimetres a year. Others travel up to one metre a day.

global warming A gradual warming of the Earth's atmosphere. Most scientists believe that this is caused by humans burning fossils fuels, such as oil and coal. The burning of these fuels gives off greenhouse gases that are trapping too much of the Sun's heat in the Earth's atmosphere.

gravity A natural force that pulls objects together. The bigger an object is, the more gravitational force it has. Earth's gravity causes objects to fall towards it.

greenhouse gases Gases such as carbon dioxide, methane and nitrous oxide. These gases trap heat from the Sun in the Earth's atmosphere – a lot like the glass roof of a greenhouse traps the Sun's heat.

heat stroke A life threatening condition caused by spending too much time in the Sun without drinking enough water.

hurricane A severe tropical storm with heavy rains and winds that can travel at 250 kilometres per hour.

ice caps Large blankets of snow and ice that cover the Earth's poles. An ice cap can also mean a smaller ice sheet covering a mountain range.

infrared photos Photographs that show heat rays. An infrared photo shows what we would see if we could see heat instead of light.

monsoon A seasonal wind that blows in different directions at different times of year. In Asia monsoon winds usually bring very heavy rains, often causing flooding.

nitrogen The gas that makes up 78% of the Earth's atmosphere. Nitrogen is essential to plant growth.

oxygen The gas that makes up 21% of the Earth's atmosphere. Most animals need oxygen to breathe.

ozone layer Ozone is a form of oxygen. The ozone layer is a protective layer of this oxygen in the Earth's upper atmosphere. It shields our planet from the Sun's harmful rays.

polar regions Areas around the North and South Poles. The poles are cold and icy. A polar climate has an average temperature below 10°C.

precipitation Any form of water (for example, rain or snow) that reaches Earth's surface from a cloud.

radiation Rays of energy released as waves or a stream of particles. Radiation from the Sun includes the light rays we see as daylight. It also includes invisible rays such as the ultraviolet rays that cause sunburn.

saturated Holding as much water or moisture as can be absorbed.

static electricity A build up of electricity in an object. It is often caused by friction. Static electricity can build up inside a storm cloud. When it leaps to the ground, we see it as a lightning bolt.

temperate A climate that is mild – not too hot, and not too cold.

tornado A violent windstorm with a twisting, funnel-shaped cloud.

tropical storm A strong storm in the tropics (the areas close to the Equator). Tropical storms usually have winds with speeds from 63 to 118 kilometres per hour.

weather balloon A balloon used by scientists to carry instruments into the atmosphere. The instruments measure air pressure, temperature and humidity (the amount of moisture in the air).

weather buoy A floating device used to carry weather instruments on water. The instruments measure air and water temperatures, the height of waves, and the speed and direction of winds.

weather station A land-based centre equipped with instruments for observing and measuring weather. Some weather stations have equipment for predicting the weather, too.

whirlwind A whirling column of wind that is most likely to occur on hot, dry, afternoons. Whirlwinds are also called dust devils due to the dust and dirt they pick up.